Contents

KV-510-609

A job with a bang!

Imagine standing on the sides of a volcano, watching as red-hot lava explodes out of its rim. The heat is incredible, the noise is terrifying, and the ground beneath you shakes as the volcano erupts. Now imagine – it is your job to be standing there! I am a volcanologist, and this is my job.

A volcanologist's job involves travelling all over the world to see eruptions and study volcanoes. Volcanologists have to collect samples of lava and rocks such as pumice to analyse in a laboratory. We also build computer models of erupting volcanoes.

Being a volcanologist is an exciting job.

THE COOLEST JOBS ON THE PLANET

Volcanologist

Hugh Tuffen with Melanie Waldron

Raintree is an imprint of Capstone Global Library Limited, a company incorporated in England and Wales having its registered office at 7 Pilgrim Street, London, EC4V 6LB – Registered company number: 6695582

To contact Raintree please phone 0845 6044371, fax + 44 (0) 1865 312263, or email myorders@raintreepublishers.co.uk. Customers from outside the UK please telephone +44 1865 312262.

Text © Capstone Global Library Limited 2015
First published in hardback in 2014
Paperback imprint published in 2015
The moral rights of the proprietor have been asserted.

Edited by Andrew Farrow, Christine Peterson and Helen Cox Cannons
Designed by Cynthia Akiyoshi
Original illustrations © Capstone Global Library Limited 2014
Illustrated by HL Studios
Picture research by Mica Brancic and Tracy Cummins
Production by Helen McCreath
Originated by Capstone Global Library Limited
Printed and bound in China

ISBN 978 1 406 28012 8 (hardback)
18 17 16 15 14
10 9 8 7 6 5 4 3 2 1

ISBN 978 1 406 28017 3 (paperback)
19 18 17 16 15
10 9 8 7 6 5 4 3 2 1

British Library Cataloguing in Publication Data
A full catalogue record for this book is available from the British Library.

Acknowledgements
We would like to thank the following for permission to reproduce photographs: Alamy pp. 14 (Pictures Colour Library/© Travel Pictures), 17 (© Arctic Images/Ragnar Th Sigurdsson); C. Ian Schipper p. 5; Getty Images pp. 4 (Perspectives/Carl Shaneff), 18 (DigitalGlobe), 37 (Christie Goodwin); Hugh Tuffen pp. 6, 7, 8, 9 bottom, 9 top, 11 bottom, 11 top, 12, 13, 19 bottom, 20, 21, 22, 23, 24, 25, 26, 27, 28, 29, 30, 31 bottom, 31 top, 32, 33, 34, 38. 39; Jeffrey A. Karson p. 36; Martin Rietze p. 15; Mike R James pp. 40, 41; Rosanna Smith p. 35; Shutterstock pp. 19 top (sunsinger), 42 chair (OZaiachin), 42 clock (Jeff Lueders), 42 microscope (Prasolov Alexei), 42 middle rock (Apollofoto), 42 rocks (Viktoria), 43 backpack (Sergey A. Kravchenko), 43 books (Quang Ho), 43 calculator (Artur Synenko), 43 hand (DenisNata). Design elements Shutterstock.

Cover photo of a volcanologist standing over a volcano reproduced with permission of Getty Images/National Geographic.

Every effort has been made to contact copyright holders of material reproduced in this book. Any omissions will be rectified in subsequent printings if notice is given to the publisher.

All the Internet addresses (URLs) given in this book were valid at the time of going to press. However, due to the dynamic nature of the Internet, some addresses may have changed, or sites may have changed or ceased to exist since publication. While the author and publisher regret any inconvenience this may cause readers, no responsibility for any such changes can be accepted by either the author or the publisher.

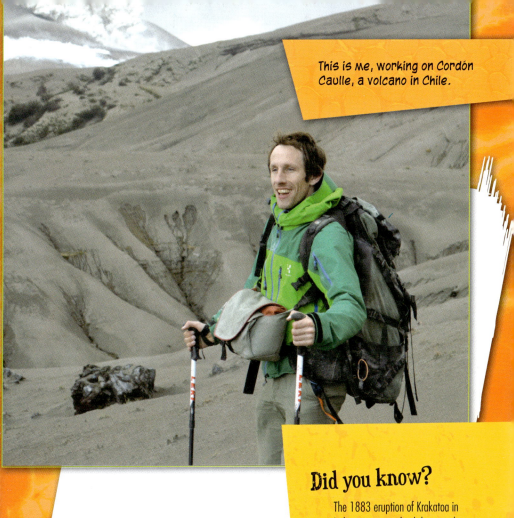

This is me, working on Cordón Caulle, a volcano in Chile.

Did you know?

The 1883 eruption of Krakatoa in Indonesia was so loud that people heard it 4,653 kilometres (2,891 miles) away. It may have made the loudest sound in human history!

There are over 500 dangerous volcanoes around the world. As you are reading this, about 20 are erupting! Millions of people can be affected by volcanic eruptions. My job as a volcanologist is to help to forecast when volcanoes are going to blow.

My job also involves studying what happens after a volcano has erupted.
I look at the type of lava and ash that the volcano throws out. I help people to understand how the lava and ash will move and affect them. People working on volcanoes are specially trained to watch out for dangers and keep themselves safe.

How I became a volcanologist

My fascination with rocks – and volcanoes – started early. I grew up in the north of Cumbria, a county in the north of England. I loved to go walking and climbing on nearby hills, called fells. When I was a teenager, I was amazed to learn from a book that many of the fells were actually extinct volcanoes. I never realized that I had been walking over lava and ash for all these years. This first sparked my interest in volcanoes.

This is me as a 10-year-old on top of a fell in Cumbria, with my dog Liffey.

TOOLS OF THE TRADE:

Volcanologists need to enjoy science! Physics and chemistry are especially important. It is also a good idea to study maths. Some of my work involves working with data and presenting it correctly.

School and university

At my school – Cockermouth School in Cumbria – I had some great science teachers. I did well in my exams and decided to carry on studying at university. Part of my course involved studying an extinct volcano on the Scottish island of Arran. Standing inside this long-dead volcano, looking at the amazing rock formations, and thinking about the way they came about – I was hooked!

I got my degree in Geology in 1997 and then decided to study for a Masters degree in Volcanology, in France. I saw my first ever volcanic eruption on Mount Etna in Italy. I will never forget watching from the crater edge as huge chunks of lava were blasted high into the sky above us.

This is me on holiday in Reykjavík, Iceland, after I completed my Masters degree. Iceland is a place I have visited many times during my career.

My first big research project

After I finished my Masters degree, I decided to apply to Lancaster University to study for a PhD – a higher degree called a Doctorate – in Volcanology. I was really keen to study a mysterious volcano in Iceland called Torfajökull [pronounced TOR-vah-yo-kutl], shown here. It has produced some enormous eruptions, yet few people have studied it and no one has seen it erupt. I was thrilled to be offered the chance to study what had happened during some of its biggest eruptions, working alongside some top volcanologists.

NOTE TO SELF

It's important to take a tarpaulin sheet for camping on a volcano. It can be so useful: as a tent groundsheet; as a shelter from rain or falling ash; as a windbreak; or even as a sledge for sliding down snowy slopes!

Now for the science...

The fieldwork was not just about having fun in amazing locations! We had to work out some puzzling things about the volcano's eruptions. There were some exciting moments when we discovered some extraordinary cracks inside lava flows that nobody had ever described before. I remember getting goosebumps when I realized that these cracks could explain a long-standing mystery – exactly how earthquakes can be triggered inside volcanoes.

At the edge of a lava flow, there are natural hot pools to swim in. I made some great friends in Iceland, and decided I had the best job in the world.

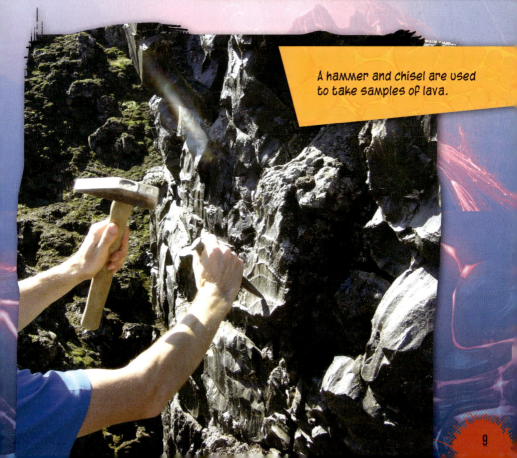

A hammer and chisel are used to take samples of lava.

Exciting new projects

After my work on Torfajökull, I wrote all my findings into a long report called a thesis. In 2002, I became Dr Hugh Tuffen.

I spent some time back in Iceland helping scientists monitor some active volcanoes. Then I moved to Munich in Germany, to work with one of the world's best teams of volcano researchers. From there, I studied one of the most explosive volcanic eruptions ever – at Taupo in New Zealand.

This map shows the locations of places mentioned in this book. The black triangles are volcanoes.

Iceland
Hrafntinnusker | Torfajökull
Eyjafjallajökull Katla
Arran Cumbria
Lancaster UK
Germany
Munich
Mount Vesuvius Italy
Mount Etna
Mount St Helens
USA
Kilauea
Japan
Mount Unzen
Indonesia
Krakatoa
Chile
Cordon Caulle
Volcan Osorno
Taupo
New Zealand

Testing my ideas

After studying Taupo, I returned to the UK to test an idea that I had. I heated up pieces of lava in the laboratory, then smashed them up. I used my results to work out that when huge cracks form in lava inside volcanoes, earthquakes can be triggered. This discovery has helped volcanologists like me to understand what happens inside volcanoes before eruptions.

My hero!
Dave McGarvie (born 1957)

Dave McGarvie is a Scottish volcanologist who was my supervisor for my PhD. He is a fountain of knowledge on Icelandic volcanoes. He has taught me a great deal about fieldwork and eruptions under ice. He also passed on lots of great tips for camping on remote snowy volcanoes. For example, he told me about cooking rice in a boiling mudpot, and about organizing my days so that there's time for a great toboggan ride back to the campsite!

This is a piece of Icelandic lava after I smashed it to pieces in the lab (inset).

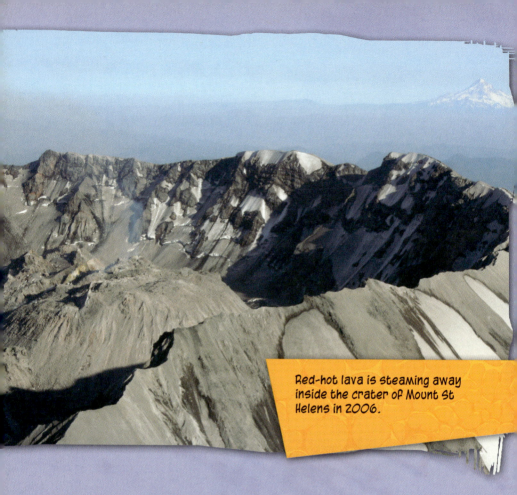

Red-hot lava is steaming away inside the crater of Mount St Helens in 2006.

Working on Mount St Helens

The next big volcano project I worked on was on Mount St Helens, in Washington, USA, from 2006. This volcano had erupted in 1980, killing 57 people. We got the chance to fly right over the top of the volcano's crater in a tiny aeroplane, in order to photograph the crater and the growing pile of lava.

During this trip, one of our camping sites was inside the crater of the volcano as it was erupting. This was really exciting but definitely scary! I woke up in the middle of the night to hear the sound of rocks breaking. I jumped out of my tent, thinking a major explosion had started. But the noise was just a huge part of a cliff beneath our campsite that was collapsing.

Realizing I could help save lives

I visited Mount Unzen in Japan in 2007. The volcano was erupting between 1990 and 1995. When I was there, I saw how the volcanologists working there could help save lives. They were constantly measuring and monitoring the volcano. They were able to warn people to leave the area when they thought the volcano was becoming dangerous.

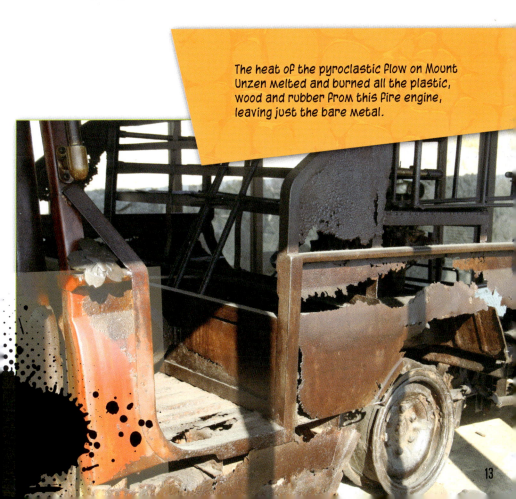

The heat of the pyroclastic flow on Mount Unzen melted and burned all the plastic, wood and rubber from this fire engine, leaving just the bare metal.

Volcano alert: why we need volcanologists

Throughout history, there have been some huge, devastating volcanic eruptions, killing thousands of people. Part of the work that I do is to try to help protect people from volcanic eruptions.

Mount Vesuvius, Italy

A surprise eruption

Almost 2,000 years ago near Naples, Italy, Mount Vesuvius erupted. A huge pyroclastic flow engulfed the whole area. Thousands of people were buried alive. Today, over four million people live nearby Mount Vesuvius – and it is likely to erupt again in the near future.

Volcanologists are using computer models to predict which areas are threatened by pyroclastic flows and lavas from Mount Vesuvius. They are also measuring earthquakes and gases at the volcano to detect any changes in its behaviour.

Grounding air travel

In 2010, a volcano called Eyjafjallajökull [pronounced AY-yah-FYAH-dlah-YER-kutl] erupted in Iceland. A huge ash cloud drifted towards Europe. This led to enormous disruption to air travel around the world, as aircraft engines can be damaged by ash. Hundreds of thousands of flights were cancelled, leaving many travellers stranded.

After the eruption of Eyjafjallajökull, many scientists became convinced that it was important to study Icelandic volcanoes.

Did you know?

The pyroclastic flow from Mount Vesuvius dumped up to 18 metres (60 feet) of ash and pumice on the people living in the Roman towns of Pompeii and Herculaneum. In the 19th century, archaeologists working on the sites found hollows in the ash. These showed where the bodies had lain before decaying away.

Hazardous volcanoes

Many of the world's volcanoes are closely monitored by volcanologists and other scientists. However, there are many volcanoes in places such as Indonesia and Latin America that are still not properly monitored. Different volcanoes are hazardous in different ways.

Some volcanoes release clouds of ash that sweep down their sides, destroying everything in their path. Other volcanoes send enormous ash plumes into the sky. Red-hot lava comes from many volcanoes, either as fast-flowing rivers or as thick mounds that gradually pour out of the mountain. Volcanoes can suddenly collapse, generating devastating rock avalanches and tsunamis. Ice-covered volcanoes are especially dangerous, as melting ice can trigger powerful, sudden floods.

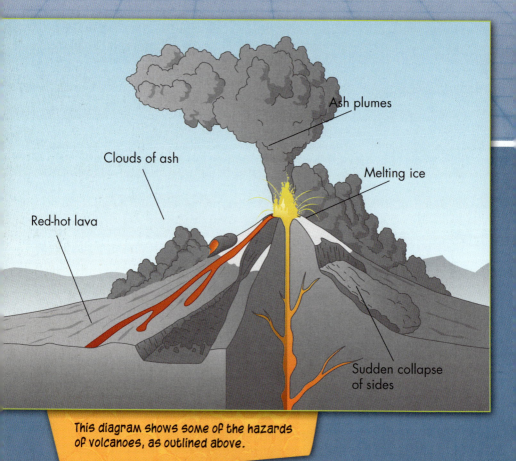

Ash plumes

Clouds of ash

Melting ice

Red-hot lava

Sudden collapse of sides

This diagram shows some of the hazards of volcanoes, as outlined above.

TOOLS OF THE TRADE: INSTRUMENTS

Volcanologists must have confidence in their instruments and be sure of their results. Telling people to evacuate when there is no real danger can be a problem, because the next time they are told to evacuate, they may decide to stay put instead. This time, however, the danger might be real.

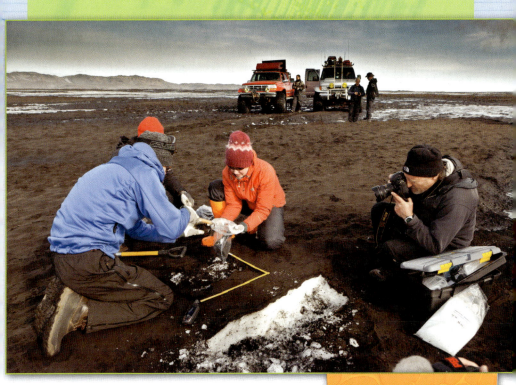

Saving lives!

A volcanologist's job is to investigate how and why volcanoes erupt. Many volcanologists work on active volcanoes, and part of their job is to help forecast when a hazardous eruption is about to start. This gives people living near the volcano time to escape the danger. Saving lives in this way is an important part of a volcanologist's job.

Volcanoes give some signs that they are about to erupt. Sometimes the ground around the volcano swells. Sometimes there are earthquakes when rocks inside the volcano crack. Many volcanoes release toxic gases from their craters. Volcanologists monitor all these things.

Volcanologists in Iceland collect ash from the powerful explosive eruption of Eyjafjallajökull. They will then take it back to the lab and analyse the shape of the ash particles to see what drove the explosions.

17

My research on volcanoes

I am very interested in explosive eruptions, where magma is ripped to pieces in powerful explosions that can blast ash high into the sky. I want to research what happens inside a volcano before the explosive eruption happens.

Changing eruptions

I am also interested in how and why volcanic eruptions suddenly change. Some volcanoes switch from powerful explosive eruptions to more gentle eruptions, when lava slowly oozes out.

In this photo, Cordón Caulle in Chile is erupting explosively. The huge ash cloud creates thunderstorms, with powerful lightning flashes.

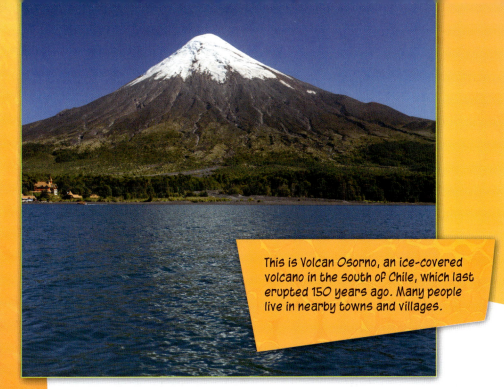

This is Volcan Osorno, an ice-covered volcano in the south of Chile, which last erupted 150 years ago. Many people live in nearby towns and villages.

Fire under ice

My final area of research involves volcanoes that lie under huge caps of ice. When they erupt, they can trigger devastating floods as the ice suddenly melts. Very little is known about these dangerous volcanoes.

TOOLS OF THE TRADE: FIELD NOTEBOOK

Although volcanologists take more and more sophisticated equipment onto volcanoes, the most useful tool is always a field notebook. I use mine to sketch the eruptions and rocks I see, write down ideas, and record any measurements that I make. Sometimes bad weather means I'm stuck in my tent for days at a time. In this case, I can also use my notebook to keep a diary and write letters to friends and family. As soon as I get home, I photocopy my whole notebook, as I'm scared of losing it! On the right is a copy of a page from my notebook written during my fieldwork in Iceland.

Studying Mount Etna

Mount Etna, in Italy, is one of the world's most active volcanoes. It erupts almost every year. I am studying what happens inside the lava as it flows down the volcano's sides. I take samples of the lava and "cook" it in the laboratory, until it is well over 1,000 degrees Celsius (1,832 degrees Fahrenheit)! Then I can study how crystals grow inside the lava as it cools, as this thickens the lava and slows it down. The results will help us to predict how far away from the volcano people will need to be evacuated.

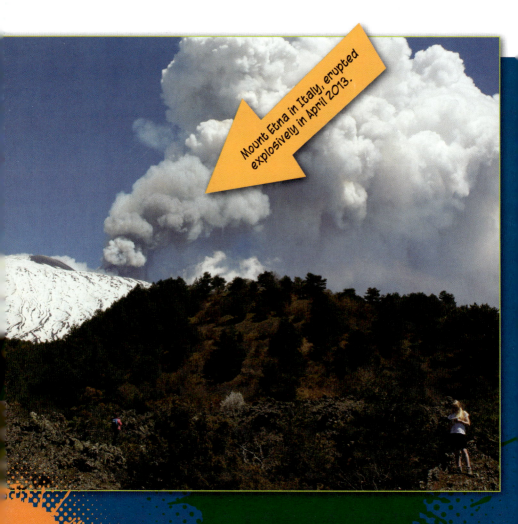

Mount Etna in Italy, erupted explosively in April 2013.

An eruption in waiting

I am also working on Katla in Iceland. It is a huge volcano, covered in ice. When it last erupted, in 1918, the ice melted extremely quickly. A huge torrent of water – more powerful than the Amazon River – poured down its sides. Many scientists are afraid that it will erupt again soon. It is such a massive volcano that an eruption could have terrible effects – much worse than at Eyjafjallajökull in 2010.

Volcanologist Jacqui Owen crosses a plain of black volcanic ash as she walks towards Katla.

Did you know?

The immense flood triggered by the 1918 Katla eruption is thought to have been up to 20 metres (66 feet) deep and moved at over 32 kilometres (20 miles) per hour. It carried enormous icebergs and boulders the size of houses. An ancient Icelandic legend says that a witch called Katla causes the eruptions, and that she possesses a magical pair of trousers that allow people to run as far as they like without getting tired!

Help from other scientists

There is so much to understand about volcanoes! Many scientists help me in my research. Each one is an expert in their area, and they all help me to understand all the different processes that are going on. Chemists help me to understand exactly what different lavas are made of, and which gases come out of volcanoes. They can measure the different elements inside the lava – for example copper and argon. Their information can help me to understand how lavas behave differently.

Tamsin Mather, a chemist and volcanologist, uses special equipment to monitor the gases coming out of volcanoes and measure their composition (what they are made of). Tamsin has found that volcanoes give off huge quantities of toxic metals such as mercury.

My hero! Magnús Tumi Guðmundsson (born 1961)

Magnús Tumi Guðmundsson is an Icelandic physicist and geologist who has made some real breakthroughs in understanding eruptions at ice-covered volcanoes. He found me a job monitoring Icelandic volcanoes after my PhD. He also lent me his best suit when I came straight from a volcano to an important meeting and only had dirty field gear to wear! We are still working together on Icelandic volcanoes.

Numbers and rocks

Physicists are scientists that use mathematics to explain how things move and change. They help me to understand what happens to lava when it cools down. I work with a physicist to model lava flows on computers. We can use these models to work out where flows will go, and how fast they will move.

Geologists are experts in understanding different rocks and their properties. I work with geologists who specialize in different areas. Yan Lavallee is a rock physicist and geologist who studies how volcanic rocks flow and break. In the picture below, he is using a permeameter whilst working in Japan. This is a machine that sucks air through lava to measure how easily gas can flow and escape.

Working on volcanoes

During my fieldwork on volcanoes, I carry out many tasks, depending on the type of volcano I am working on and the research I am doing.

Ian Schipper and I stand at the foot of a lava flow in Chile, while blocks the size of tables tumble down. The lava makes extraordinary cracking noises that sound like thousands of plates being smashed.

Rivers of red rock

Volcanoes such as Mount Etna in Italy and Kilauea in Hawaii produce long rivers of lava. We can learn a lot from observing and collecting samples from lava flows. This can mean being close to red-hot lava – but not too close. I know people who have melted the soles of their boots by standing on lava that was too hot! However, not all lava is like a hot, red river – like the flow in the picture above.

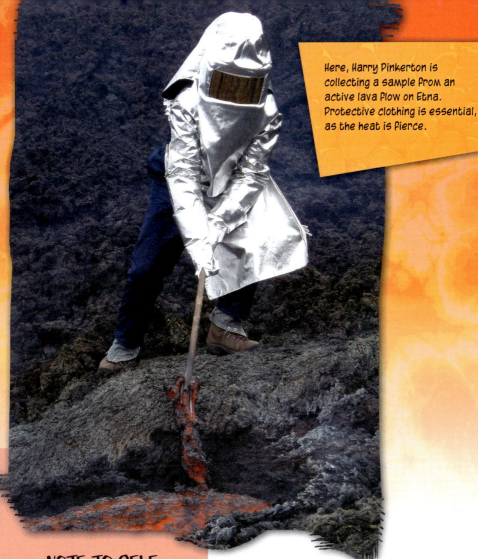

Here, Harry Pinkerton is collecting a sample from an active lava flow on Etna. Protective clothing is essential, as the heat is fierce.

NOTE TO SELF

We spend a lot of time thinking about safety and never take risks. We have plans in place in case the eruption suddenly changes, and constantly monitor the volcanic activity. You should never work alone on an active volcano.

Taking lava samples

I collect samples of lava with either a hammer or a drill. Thick gloves might be needed if the lava is still hot. Samples are usually fist-sized lumps. I note where I collect each sample, using a GPS, then I photograph and label it. After that, I chuck each sample in my rucksack (which can get heavy at the end of the day) and carry them back to camp. At the end of a field trip, I send the samples back to the UK in sturdy crates.

Collecting ash

It is really useful to collect samples of ash as it falls from a volcano, before it hits the ground or is mixed with rainwater. With this ash, you know exactly when it was blasted out of the ground, and all the chemicals in it are fresh. The ash cools as it falls and can be collected on paper or even brushed from our tents.

TOOLS OF THE TRADE: CAMERA

I always take a good camera on my fieldwork trips. It is very useful to film explosive eruptions. This is because you can then watch them over and over again, examining how often and how high the explosions appear, and learning a lot about what controls them. We can even make 3D models of the shape of a lava flow using photographs!

Jon Castro and Ian Skilling watch the ash plume at Cordón Caulle in 2012, from a safe distance. We could see blocks of lava the size of cars being blasted into the air.

Staying out of harm's way

When I work on volcanoes that are erupting, I have to be very careful where I set up camp. It has to be on high ground, in a place where pyroclastic flows can't reach it and where dangerous volcanic gases can't gather. It has to be far enough from the crater that no large pieces of lava or pumice can fall on it. It also has to have a view of the crater so that I can see if the volcanic activity suddenly increases.

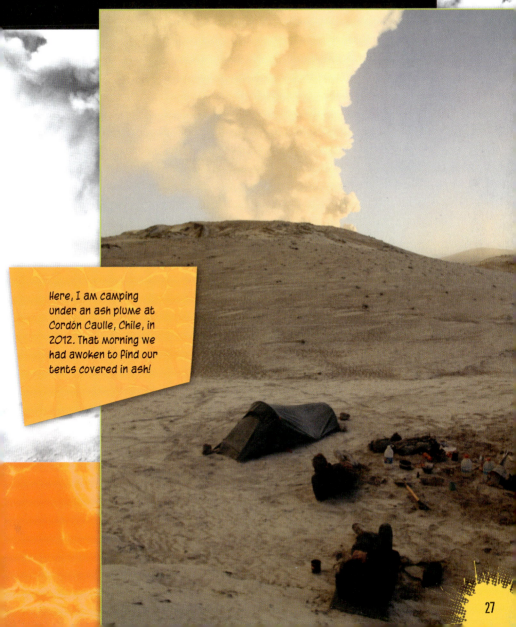

Here, I am camping under an ash plume at Cordón Caulle, Chile, in 2012. That morning we had awoken to find our tents covered in ash!

Ancient volcanoes

Detective work on ancient volcanoes can tell us all kinds of things about how volcanoes behave and what happens inside them. Eruptions in the past have created layers of lavas and ash that we can now safely study. We can work out amazing things about what happened thousands or even millions of years ago in the world's biggest eruptions. It's like visiting a crime scene and trying to work out the puzzle of whodunnit!

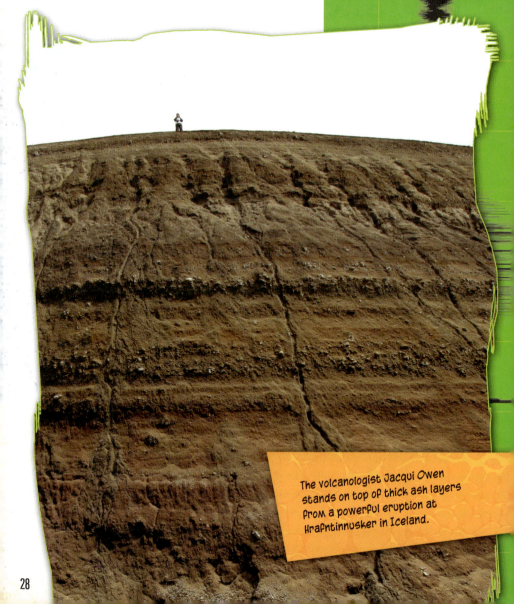

The volcanologist Jacqui Owen stands on top of thick ash layers from a powerful eruption at Hrafntinnusker in Iceland.

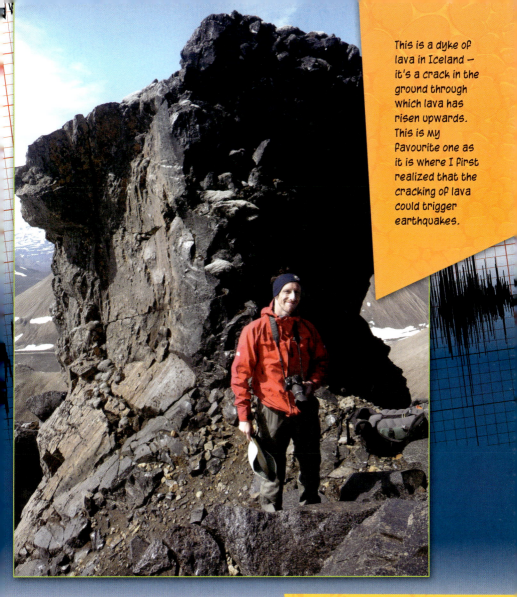

This is a dyke of lava in Iceland – it's a crack in the ground through which lava has risen upwards. This is my favourite one as it is where I first realized that the cracking of lava could trigger earthquakes.

Getting inside volcanoes

I love working on old volcanoes that have been cut into by rivers and glaciers. You can see right inside these volcanoes and learn how lava rose to the surface through cracks in the volcano. When I am working on old volcanoes I never forget my field notebook (see page 19), so I can sketch the rocks I see and draw cartoons of what I think happened during the eruption.

Did you know?

There are many volcanoes on Earth, but the biggest volcano in the solar system is on Mars. This volcano is called Olympus Mons, and it is almost 624 kilometres (388 miles) wide and 25 kilometres (16 miles) high.

Fieldwork is a big part of my job – and I love it! I usually go on two or three big expeditions every year, mostly to Iceland or Chile. I sometimes go to other places too, such as Japan, Italy and the United States. Here is what a typical day is like for me.

7.00 a.m.	Wake up, collect water from a nearby spring, make porridge and coffee for breakfast with my volcanologist friends
8.30 a.m.	Put my boots on (after first emptying all the ash that might have fallen in the day before!) and walk for a couple of hours to an advancing lava flow
10.30 a.m	Arrive at the lava flow and take photographs and measurements
1.00 p.m.	Have lunch next to the lava (but not too close!)

It is breakfast time at our campsite at Cordón Caulle.

1.30 p.m.	Hike to some interesting ash deposits
2.00 p.m.	Take samples of ash
5.00 p.m.	Walk back to the campsite
6.30 p.m.	Arrive at camp and cook a huge meal for everyone
8.00 p.m.	Discuss discoveries with other volcanologists, watch the eruption from our campsite and look at the stars once night has fallen
10.00 p.m.	Head to my tent and sleep like a log

NOTE TO SELF

Don't forget: tent, sleeping bag, camping stove, hammer, sample bags, warm clothes, goggles, sunglasses, first aid kit, rope, tarpaulin, torch, sun cream, camera, solar panel, notebook, several litres of drinking water if needed, rice, vegetables, tinned fish, nuts, dried fruit, chocolate. Luxury items: MP3 player, book, sweets!

We prepare the evening meal by torchlight.

Our team climbs the ash-covered slope of Cordón Caulle.

Volcanoes in the lab

When I get home from fieldwork, I try to recreate what happens in volcanic eruptions in the laboratory. This helps me to understand things such as how lava moves, and how it gets frothy and cools to form pumice.

In my lab, I have a special furnace that allows me to cook lava and film what happens through a powerful microscope. I use this to study how crystals and bubbles grow in lava.

Laboratory equipment

We need special equipment to do our experiments. We need furnaces that can reach 1,500 degrees Celsius (2,732 degrees Fahrenheit), and microphones that we use to record the sound waves made when we smash rocks.

Toasting lava

I also have two bits of equipment that look a bit like toasters! I use these to heat up lava and dry it out. I capture and measure the gases, such as water vapour and carbon dioxide, that are given off as the lava dries out. This helps me to understand a lot about the gases that move inside volcanoes.

This is lava, seen through the microscope. These pictures are less than 1 millimetre across. As the hot lava (top left) cools, crystals form (bottom right) and we can measure how quickly they grow.

RECIPE FOR PUMICE

You need: a pea-sized chunk of lava, sandpaper, a furnace.

1. Collect a piece of lava from a volcano in Iceland.
2. Hand polish the lava until it is no thicker than a piece of paper.
3. Place a tiny piece in the furnace.
4. Heat to 850 °C (1,562 °F) for 5 minutes.
5. Cool quickly and serve!

Detecting chemicals

Understanding what lava and ash are made of is really important. Volcanologists think that gases trapped inside lava, especially water vapour and carbon dioxide, are what creates the pressure that makes volcanoes go BANG!

I work with students at Lancaster University and many of them are involved in measuring the gases in volcanic rocks. They use amazing equipment to test ideas about what controls eruptions.

There is a competition between us to get to use the most advanced kit to measure chemicals, and if you're a lucky winner you need to make the most of the kit! When Ellen, Jacqui and I got the chance to shine the UK's most powerful light beam through our lava samples to measure chemicals, we worked in shifts around the clock for four days and collected thousands of measurements.

My PhD student Ellen McGowan is using an incredibly powerful beam of light made by a huge machine called a synchrotron. She is shining the light beam, which is narrower than a human hair, through Icelandic lava to measure the chemicals that it contains. This is helping her work out what controls explosive eruptions in Iceland.

Rock-breaking work

Finding out how rocks break apart is also really important in understanding volcanoes. Eruptions start when cracks form in the rocks inside volcanoes and lava starts to rise through these cracks to the surface. We are trying to work out how much pressure is needed for rocks to break, and how this links to the earthquakes that occur just before rocks break. Some of my students break lava in the lab using specialist, hand-built equipment found nowhere else in the world.

20cm

TOOLS OF THE TRADE: HIGH TEMPERATURE TRIAXIAL PRESS

We use a piece of equipment called a high-temperature triaxial press. It has a metal rod called a piston that can put 25 tonnes (27.5 tons) of pressure onto a piece of rock the size of your thumb. This is equal to having 3.5 elephants standing on your thumb! This all happens inside a furnace that goes up to 1,000 degrees Celsius (1,832 degrees Fahrenheit).

Pouring lava!

It is fun and interesting to work with real lava at incredibly high temperatures. But we have to be very careful – it can also be dangerous. At Syracuse University in the United States, some volcanologists have made amazing lava flows. They melt a huge amount of lava in an outdoor furnace and pour it onto sand and ice. They film the lava up close and measure its temperature. It must be exciting to make a lava flow at the touch of a button!

Did you know?

Hot lava is strange stuff. It doesn't know if it is a solid or a liquid. If you squeeze it slowly, it oozes like thick, hot toothpaste. But squash it very quickly and it will shatter like glass. Lava can both shatter and flow inside volcanoes, sometimes at the same time.

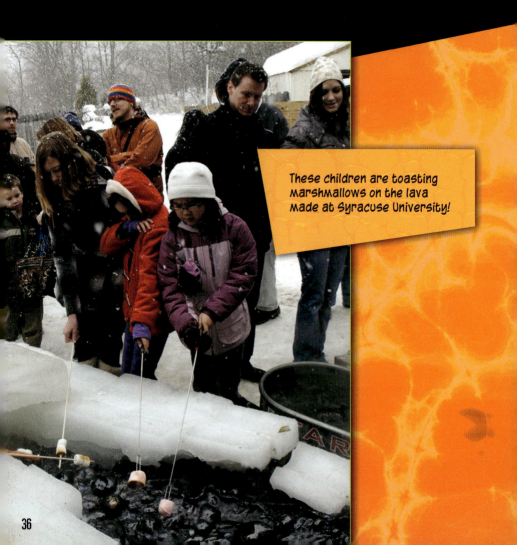

These children are toasting marshmallows on the lava made at Syracuse University!

Sweet-tasting lava!

In our experiments, it can sometimes be safer and easier to use something in place of lava. It needs to be thick and gloopy, and move like lava does. One of our favourite things to use is golden syrup. It is the correct thickness and gloopiness, and it behaves a little like runny lava. Some of my colleagues have used enormous tanks of it to examine how lava flows and how bubbles move through it. I wish I could have put some of it on my fieldwork porridge!

Irish comedian Ed Byrne helped volcanologists send bubbles through a tube of golden syrup during a television programme about volcanoes in 2012.

A day in the office

There is a huge contrast between the work I do in the office and fieldwork. In the office, I have a shorter working day so that I can spend time with my children. When I am doing fieldwork, the working days can be really long, and the expeditions can take weeks. My children will not be joining me on my fieldwork trips until they are in their teens!

6.45 a.m.	Wake up, prepare breakfast
8.15 a.m.	Cycle to university nursery, where I drop off the children
9.00 a.m.	Read emails and latest volcano news
10.00 a.m.	Go to lab and start new lava cooking experiment
10.45 a.m.	Coffee with the volcanology team
11.30 a.m.	Meet with a student and discuss project on Icelandic volcanoes
12.30 p.m.	Lunch

1.30 p.m.	Write up some results about an eruption in Chile, have a new idea, talk on Skype with a colleague in Germany
4.00 p.m.	Back to lab and check experiment, record results
4.45 p.m.	Collect children from nursery, cycle home
5.30–8.00 p.m.	Spend time with my family
8.00–10.00 p.m.	Play cello with my band, rehearsing for a gig

NOTE TO SELF

Many people across the world are interested in volcanoes — especially erupting ones. Another part of my job is to talk about volcanoes — on TV, radio, and for magazines and newspapers. At first, speaking live on radio to many thousands of people was nerve-wracking. But now I really love the chance to share my enthusiasm with other people. I always remind myself to practise how to pronounce some tricky volcano names, such as Eyjafjallajökull, Sakurajima and Popocatepetl!

How to become a volcanologist

Being a volcanologist is a cool job! But you have to be prepared to study and train to do the job. Maths, physics, chemistry, geography and geology are all really useful subjects for future volcanologists.

Higher education

You need to get a university degree in order to become a volcanologist. You could choose to do a degree in Geology, Geography, Environmental Science, Physics or Chemistry. But that's not all! You also need to do a higher degree, called a Masters, in Volcanology. We run this course at Lancaster University, where I work.

Putting in the hours

After getting a Masters degree in Volcanology, you could perhaps volunteer to work for free at a volcano observatory, or with a volcano research team. This will give you great experience, and will help you get a paid job.

Some people also go on to do a PhD – a doctorate. They spend three or four years (or longer!) researching a particular subject in Volcanology. Eventually the aim is to get a great job, doing what you love, while being paid!

TOOLS OF THE TRADE: WALKING BOOTS

A good pair of walking boots is essential if you want to spend some time clambering about on volcanoes. Sometimes I have got through two pairs in one year! However, you won't be spending all your time outdoors. Much of your work as a volcanologist is spent in the lab and on the computer. So make sure you enjoy desk work, too.

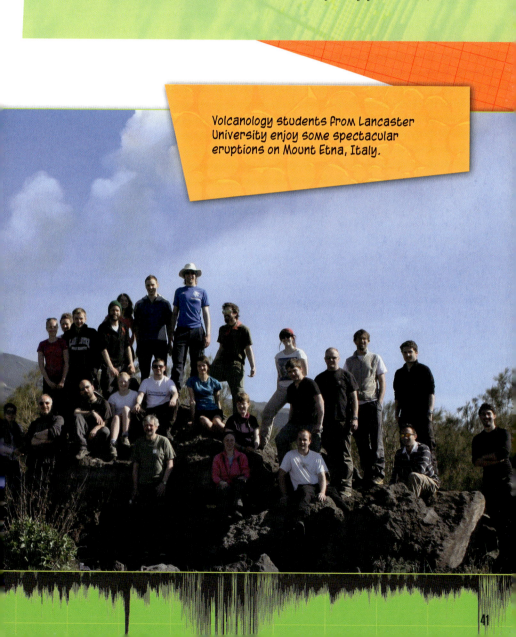

Volcanology students from Lancaster University enjoy some spectacular eruptions on Mount Etna, Italy.

Quiz

Try this quiz to see if you have what it takes to become a volcanologist!

1. On a beach, which of these things would you like to do best?

a) Lie in the sun and read your book

b) Play beach games and go swimming

c) Look through the sand and cliffs for interesting stones and rocks

2. If your sleep is interrupted...

a) You just can't get back to sleep at all and are really tired the next day

b) Nothing can wake you up – you are such a deep sleeper

c) You don't mind – you will just get back to sleep again

3. What would be your ideal workplace?

a) A busy office with lots of people coming and going, where you do the same things every day

b) A factory or workshop where you can make things with your hands

c) A laboratory where you can do experiments

4. If someone asked you to walk far, then up a mountain, carrying a large heavy rucksack…

a) You would say no

b) You would do it, but would moan and grumble all the way

c) You wouldn't mind – you like to keep fit anyway

5. How do you feel about studying hard and taking exams?

a) I'd rather not!

b) I prefer to make things rather than study things

c) I don't mind learning about things that really interest me and I am prepared to study hard for my exams

If you answered mostly Cs, you just might have what it takes to begin exploring a career as a volcanologist!

Glossary

active an active volcano is one that has erupted at least once during the last 10,000 years

archaeologist scientist who studies past human lives, especially by examining objects such as pottery, tools and buildings

ash tiny fragments of jagged rock, minerals and volcanic glass that look like soft, grey, powdery dust

composition way in which a whole or mixture is made up

computer model program run on a computer that simulates what might happen in real life

crater bowl-shaped opening at the top of a volcano

dyke large slab of rock that cuts through another type of rock

element one of the 107 basic substances that can combine with other substances to make other things; for example, water is made of hydrogen combined with oxygen

extinct an extinct volcano is one that has not erupted for at least 10,000 years and is not expected to erupt again

forecast predict

furnace an enclosed structure, like an oven, in which materials are heated to very high temperatures

geology study of the structure of Earth and how it has changed over time; geologists study rocks to find this out

GPS (Global Positioning System) system that uses satellites to pinpoint an exact location on Earth's surface

lava hot, melted rock that erupts from inside a volcano or along a crack in the ground

magma hot, molten rock that rises within volcanoes

monitor study something in order to keep a check on it to see if it changes

PhD often called a doctorate, it is based on at least three years of study on top of a normal university degree and is the highest degree awarded

physics science that looks at matter and energy, and how they are related; it includes the study of light, heat, sound, electricity and force

plain large, flat area of land

plume cloud of gas and fine particles

pressure amount of force upon a surface

pumice lava that has hardened to form a light, porous rock, a bit like a hard sponge

pyroclastic flow flow of volcanic ash, dust, rocks and debris that rushes down the slope of a volcano during an eruption; they are very dangerous, reaching enormous speeds and temperatures

solar system system that includes a star and all of the things that orbit it, including planets and their moons

thesis very long essay based on research or study, which students write as part of an advanced academic degree

toxic poisonous

tsunami very large sea wave caused by an undersea earthquake or volcanic eruption; these can cause lots of destruction when they hit land

Find out more

Books

Be a Volcanologist (Using Science), Suzy Gazlay (Ticktock, 2008)

Into the Fire: Volcanologists (Scientists at Work), Paul Mason (Heinemann Library, 2008)

Volcano Disasters (Catastrophe!), John Hawkins (Franklin Watts, 2012)

Volcanologists and Seismologists (Out of the Lab: Extreme Jobs in Science), Ruth Owen (PowerKids Press, 2013)

Websites

http://www.bbc.co.uk/news/science-environment-24821494

This BBC news story is a commentary about the lava flow at Cordón Caulle in Chile.

www.bbc.co.uk/programmes/p00v4wkb

You can see a short film I made about the erupting volcano Puyehue in Chile, and other short clips all about volcanoes.

kids.discovery.com/games/build-play/volcano-explorer

This fun website allows you to create your own volcano and watch it erupt.

volcanoes.usgs.gov

On this website, there is a huge amount of information, games, videos and photos.

**www.nhm.ac.uk/kids-only/earth-space/volcanoes/
build-a-volcano**

Build your own volcano on the Natural History Museum
website.

Topic for research

There is a lot you can find out about before you decide to
become a volcanologist. Go into your local library and find
all the books you can on volcanoes. Read them and try to
understand as much as you can about them. Look out for
any news stories about volcanoes around the world, and find
out what volcanologists are doing in these places.

Index